Sweet Sixteen

Poems by

Pamela Martin

Sweet Sixteen
Copyright 2009 by Pamela Gowan

All rights reserved under International and Pan-American copyright conventions. No part of this book may be reproduced, stored in a retrieval system or transmitted in any form, electronic, mechanical, or by any other means, without written permission of the author.

International Standard Book Number: 978-0-578-01421-0

Illustrated by Kathleen Hardy.

Table of Contents

Part I

Divination 9
"Love is blind" 9
Judge Judith Scheindlin 9
Futurism 10
Practically My Father 10
Awesome! 10
Loosely Tethered 11
"Dial America" 12
Hoof-in-mouth Disease 12
"Fire in the Hole" 12
Necromancy 13
Q & A 14
The School Bored 14
"Cut to the Chase" 14
"Tomorrow, and tomorrow, and tomorrow…" 15
"Death be not Proud" 16
"On the Ledgie" 16
"Filly me up!" 16
Pirate's Plunder 17
Fool Hardy 18
Lake Eerie 18
Paying My Dues 18
Beau Brummell 19
Halcyon Pam 20
Robbing the Cradles 20
"Unsterbliche Geliebte" 20
Fealty 21
Circular Reasoning 21
Malicious Persecution 21
A Plutonic Relationship 22
Crumbs 22
"Might Makes Right" 22
The Doldrums 23
Alone Together 23
"Manifest Destiny" 23
Enlightened Self-Interest 24

Part II

Anthropocentric Knowledge 27
A Wise Guy 27
Baby Einstein 27
"Decon" 28
The Lunar Eclipse 28
Standard Deductions 28
Naturally Induced Hedonism 29
The Chase 30
D.N.A. 30
The Fallen Sparrow 30
Decomposed 31
The Truth Machine or Lie Detector 32
Above the Fray 32
Recitative 32
Double Speak 33
Swinging the Blues 34
"I Will" 34
"Endless Love" 34
Fondly 35
The Expectorant 36
A Bucolic Landscape 36
"Stat!" 36
Act Now! 37
Courageous to a Fault 38
James Abbott McNeill "It ain't worth a farthing" Whistler 38
An Unexamined Life 39
Temper Temper 39
A Commissioned Omission 39
The Equinox 40
Christian Ethics 40
"(Proud to) Be an American" 40
Criminal Minds 41
The Old Maid New 41
Pathology 41
The Messenger 42

Part III

A Bad Childhood	45
Abroad is a Broad	45
Taking Sides	45
The Key of Life	46
Introversion	46
The Individualist	46
"Sixteen Candles"	47
A Wrongful Death	48
An Open Door Policy	48
The Good, the Bad, and the Cogent	48
"Gosh Darn It!"	49
A Queen Anne	50
Organ Failure	50
De profundis	50
My Mistress	51
The Bankrupted Divorcee	52
Pearl Vision	52
Not a Chance	52
"Stuffed Mushrooms"	53
Horse Sense	54
A Woman Scorned	54
"Game Point"	54
Demigod	55
"Freedom is not free"	56
"Suspended Animation"	56
Interlocution	56
Eternal Bleeding	57
"You had me at 'Hello'"	57
The Gift You Keep on Giving	57
Creative Orthography	58
Continuous Discontinuity	58
Disorderly Conduct	58
Agnes Dei	59
Re-Parenting 101	59
"Hallucinogenic Spores"	59
Fact Checking	60

Part I

Divination

I just talked to my best friend.
I got a contact high.
But it won't last the whole day through.
I do not know why,
Why we can't be happy,
Happy all the time.
Then we would approach
The utterly divine.

"Love is blind"

"I see," said the blind man
As he picked up his hammer and saw.
And that would have to be,
Murphy's "golden" law.
If you were blind
What would you see?
The hammer and the sickle
Or would you see me?

Judge Judith Scheindlin

My father watches *Judge Judy*
Each and every day.
Never does he ever
Let anything get in the way
Of her majesty's presence
In that noble court.
Everyone loves Judge Judy
I am happy to report.

Futurism

The more superficial we are
The deeper we get.
And never will they ever
Let us forget
We are orphans
With few ties
To the past.
It's no surprise.

Practically My Father

My dad is an enabler.
He helps me
To be all
I can be.
Without him
I'd be lost.
I could do it alone
But at what cost?

Awesome!

Clinically creative
I am not.
Those rules of grammar
I forgot.
But when it comes
To my theory,
I have a wonderful
Philosophy.

Loosely Tethered

I thank my lucky stars!
(If what they say is true)
I found the loveliest person
When I met you.
Now I go through the day
Thinking of when
Our true love
Will finally begin.

"Dial America"

I believe in the efficacy of human agency
To the extent
I am successful
In paying my rent.
When I cannot,
I will be homeless.
But, worst of all,
I will be phone-less.

Hoof-in-mouth Disease

It's either fame or famine
If you ask me.
Or that's the way
It seems to be.
But "either/or" thinking
Will bring you down
If you don't keep
Your feet on the ground.

"Fire in the Hole"

If you want to be cremated,
Here's what you should do.
Call the Neptune Society
Before funeral expenses accrue.
Dial 1-800
581-3882
There is nothing more
You need to do.

Necromancy

My judgment has been occluded
By the simple fact
I have been deluded
By a heart attack.
I don't have to tell you
I wish I could say,
"Abracadabra,"
And it would go away.

Q & A

Do you believe in destiny
Or do you believe in pre-destiny?
I do my best to try to ignore
Things that have come before.
Does your conscience ever tinge
When you go on another binge?
Moderation, dear, is for the monks
And that is a "slam dunk."
Does the sun rise and set?
That would be my best bet.
Do you think I love only you?
Only if you want me to.

The School Bored

I have come to the conclusion
That it is a delusion
That a sweet infusion
Of knowledge will ensue
With the proper training
As it were pertaining
To those who are remaining
Smoking in the loo.

"Cut to the Chase"

I know you know I loved you.
You know I knew it, too.
But what else is a girl
Really supposed to do?
Sit off in a corner
And pine away in vain
Or chase the little bastard
As if she were insane?

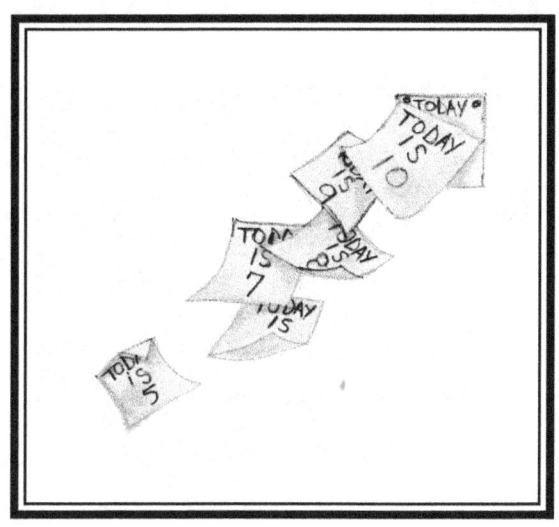

"Tomorrow, and tomorrow, and tomorrow…"*

The denunciation
Of procrastination
Is the creation
Of the clinically insane.
Put off until tomorrow
All of your sorrow.
Then you don't have to wallow
Or try to explain.

*Part of the famous quotation from Shakespeare's tragedy, *Macbeth*, that "Scottish play:"
"Tomorrow, and tomorrow, and tomorrow/Creeps in this petty pace from day to day/To that last syllable of recorded time;…"

"Death be not Proud"

Death is yet a part of us
Even as we live.
It tells us when to hold on
And when to forgive.
We experience it many times
As we go through life
And makes it more bearable
To endure our strife.

"On the Ledgie"

I agree I would not be
If I wasn't "edgy"
To the extent that I am not
A misguided little veggie.
I eat meat. It is so sweet.
Put me in the hedgie.
If I fail to wassail,
Just give me a wedgie.

"Filly me up!"

I hear the clock ticking,
Ticking in my soul.
What will I do
When I achieve my goal?
Is life worth living
In this dusty bowl?
I still have much to learn.
I am but a foal.

Pirate's Plunder

I feel I plagiarize
Every word I write.
Are they mine to utter
Or do I laconically recite
The one who first spoke them
At the beginning of time?
I simply abuse them
To make this silly rhyme.

Fool Hardy

I know that my heart
Doesn't have a clue
About what would be the only
Proper thing to do
In a situation
Where he has been untrue.
I would have to tell him
He has been a fool.

Lake Eerie

Would it be enough for you
To steal my heart away
And return it promptly
To the layaway?
It really makes me wonder
What you would do
If your incriminations
Came back to haunt you.

Paying My Dues

The less I know what people think,
The better off I am.
This is not something you can concur
Or even understand
Because these are the very people
I really have to thank
When I make a deposit
At the local bank.

Beau Brummell

You are the most beautiful
Person in my eyes.
Then why is it you put on
That wonderful disguise?
Think about the energy
You put into your stealth.
Are you hiding from someone
Or hiding from yourself?

Halcyon Pam

If the truth be known I'm all alone
Living in this hell.
But I decry those who try
To make me so swell.
If my life seems full of peace
It only goes to show
They can't see the reality.
They will never know.

Robbing the Cradles

If the truth be told, I'm so old
I could be your mother.
But I'm not and soon forgot
Is your younger brother
Who I betook to be a crook.
But it really makes me wonder
What I saw in him, a passing whim.
It must have been my hunger.

*"Unsterbliche Geliebte"**

In order to attain
Immortality
You must first refrain
From immorality.
Then when you're on the way
To the undertaker,
Your face will have a place
In every newspaper.

*German, to my "Immortal Beloved," a love letter addressed (probably to Antoine von Birkenstock Brentano, a married woman, who Beethoven met in 1811), and was found at the time of his death in 1827.

Fealty

I do see that honesty
Is grossly understated.
But sincerity will always be
Greatly overrated.
I know you are subject to
Untrammeled emotion.
So much so you have to go
And promise your devotion.

Circular Reasoning

The dialog inside my head
Spits out vitriol
Faster than a speeding bullet
I cannot control.
The alpha and omega
Take a leaping bound.
This vertiginous circle
Just keeps spinning 'round.

Malicious Persecution

It hurts more than it helps
When you criticize.
It's vindictive to predict
Someone else's demise.
I don't want to hear
How I maligned your mother,
Your father and your sister,
And your little brother.

A Plutonic Relationship*

At times, I am funny.
At times, I'm a wit.
But I really want
Is to discomfit.
I have to say
I have said too much.
Tomorrow is another day
When you're out to lunch.

*Refers to Pluto, the binary dwarf planet furthest from the Earth, that was named after the Greek (Hades) and the Roman (Pluto) god the underworld of death. It is here used to symbolize the symbiotic but "far out" relationship between the wit and the dimwit (i.e. the audience or society).

Crumbs

When it comes to making love,
It has to be
The one thing I need most
In reality.
But you only want me
To leave you alone.
I think I'm lucky
When you telephone.

"Might Makes Right"

When Tabby sees Sammy,
Sammy runs away.
But not always.
Sometimes they play.
Sammy is older
And wiser than Tab.
But Tabby is bigger
And bolder and bad.

The Doldrums

I can stretch my imagination
Farther than you.
You could if you would
But you don't want to.
Picture a perfect,
Sunny Sunday
Watching two kitties
Wander and play.

Alone Together

"A little knowledge is dangerous,"
But only if it's known
How much you know
About the unknown.
When the unknown is known
And the known is unknown,
Then we are together
When we are alone.

"Manifest Destiny"

We knew that we had made it
When we went aboard
The RMS Titanic
Which had been restored.
If this strikes in you
An old, familiar chord,
It is because you
Are terminally bored.

Enlightened Self-Interest

I have found in you
A noble savage
Who, I must admit,
I can easily manage.
I do not know how
You came to be this way.
But I do insist
That is how you will stay.

Part II

Anthropocentric Knowledge

When that last ship has sailed
Into the horizon,
I'll be here at this desk
Aggrandizing
Everything I have learned
Since time began.
And I do this wittingly
Since I am a man.

A Wise Guy

One day I'll poke my eye out
When I leave the spoon
In my cup of coffee.
It will be my doom.
King Lear gouged his own out
In a fit of rage.
And for that they call him
An "ignoble sage."

Baby Einstein

Even the slightest movement
Can catch Tabitha's eye.
A fly in the window.
A car passing by.
I don't have to tell you,
She's one smart cat.
If I could tap into
Some of that...

"Decon"*

It would be anachronistic
If I were to say to you,
The world is as flat
As a slab of tofu.
An analogy breaks down
Through inference and deduction
And when its permutations
Go down the path of destruction.

*Short for "deconstruction," which means to analyze rigorously or take apart and disassemble.

The Lunar Eclipse

I took the lunar rover
For a quick spin.
Even a fish out of water
Still has its fins.
When I stepped out,
It was as dark as night.
We were standing in the shadows
Looking for the light.

Standard Deductions

The "gifts or the Magi"
Were so magical.
But they itemized.
(How cynical)
When making a gift,
Always remember
To save the receipt
From your distemper.

Naturally Induced Hedonism

I want more out of life
Than watching T.V.,
Playing the horses,
And drinking iced tea.
But, tell me, what else could there
Possibly be?
When we are together,
It's ecstasy.

The Chase

I was once a baby.
Now I am grown up.
But, as they say,
I'm pushing my luck
Or pushing the envelope
Too far it seems.
There's nothing better
Than chasing your dreams.

D.N.A.*

I took to my teachers
When I was in school.
They sat in the bleachers
Playing it cool.
Now I am a poet
And they are but fools.
Maybe it was in
My genetic pool.

*Acronym for "d(eoxyribo) n(ucleic) a(cid)," which is, "the basic chromosome material, containing and transmitting the hereditary pattern." *Webster's New World Dictionary.*

The Fallen Sparrow

The lettuce has wilted
In the refrigerator.
I am not much
Of a prognosticator.
But it is now
So plain to see
The lettuce is now part
Of history.

Decomposed

I once was
But now I'm not.
But history
Has soon forgot
I once traveled
So insouciantly.
Now there is nothing
Left of me.

The Truth Machine or Lie Detector

They say I'm a poet.
They say I'm a cad,
Who can write a poem
That isn't half bad.
If they make you laugh,
Or they make you cry,
You must admit,
They do not lie.

Above the Fray

If my ideas
Appear to be half-baked,
It's because they are.
I am a fake.
There's no sense pretending.
There's no other way.
It does not matter
What people say.

Recitative

I went to the museum
And the symphony, too.
But what it is
I really like to do
Is to go to the opera.
It is a hoot.
But it requires
All of my loot.

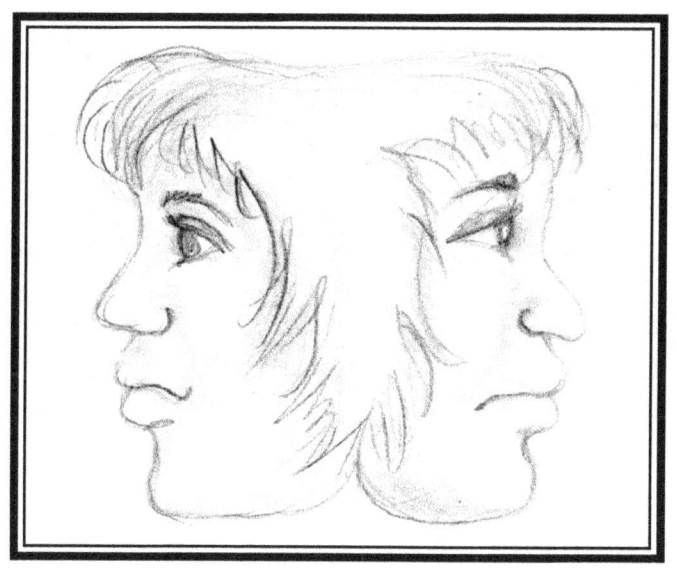

Double Speak

How can I convince you
I will be true?
What more if anything
Can I now do
To make you understand
That it was a fling
And, now that it's over,
It don't mean a thing?

Swinging the Blues

It is my job
To force creation.
It gives me
A sweet sensation
To do the thing
I ought to do
Even when
I'm feeling blue.

"I Will"*

What could be
More positive
That learning how
To live and give?
Loving you
Is greater still.
And you know
I always will.

*A motto of Chicago.

"Endless Love"

When the day
Is finally done,
I know you
Will be the one
That my eyes
Will gaze upon.
I know we will go
On and on.

Fondly

I once was
A virgin cherry
Until I met
The apothecary
Who came to town
In great style.
Now all I can do
Is smile.

The Expectorant

Tabby wears her
Long, sleek coat.
But I think
It'd be remote
That she would ever
Take it off.
If she did she'd
Get a cough.

A Bucolic Landscape

Well is all,
And all is well.
But you can
Never tell
When there will
Be a change
In the annals
Of the Grange.

"Stat!"*

The flood was caused by
Too much water
In the lowlands.
And my daughter
Drowned herself
In too much sorrow.
I can't wait
Until tomorrow.

*In a hospital, "stat" means to come immediately.

Act Now!

Each new page
Is a "gratis"
That comes out of
My epiglottis.
If you think
You can do better,
Do it now.
Don't send a letter.

Courageous to a Fault

All criticisms will
Soon be gone.
But they will
Still linger on
As I sail
Uncharted water
Where no one else
Has yet to falter.

James Abbott McNeill "It ain't worth a Farthing" Whistler*

I started
With a litany
Of things I read
In history.
That convolution
Has long since passed.
But how long
Can this "art" last?

*An American-born British painter, Whistler (b. 1834-07-14-d. 1903.), was a champion of the "art for art's sake" movement at the turn of the twentieth century. He is famous for his *Harmony in Blue and Gold: the Peacock Room* commissioned by F.R. Leyland, the "Liverpool Medici," and now in the Charles Lang Freer Gallery of Art (Smithsonian Institution), in Washington D.C. and *Arrangement in Grey and Black: the Artist's Mother* in the Musee d'Orsay in Paris. To make a long story short, I call him "It ain't worth a Farthing" Whistler because Whistler sued John Ruskin, a famous nineteenth century British art critic, for libel for opining that one of his painting (all of his paintings) wasn't worth a farthing (a penny). "Millions for defense but not a farthing for a Whistler," wrote Ruskin (hyperbolically speaking). Whistler, who strutted about the courtroom like a peacock, won the case but was symbolically awarded only "a farthing."

An Unexamined Life

She lies there
With sleepy eyes.
So unconcerned
I realize
She has not
A single care.
She goes through life
So unaware.

Temper Temper

I wrote that poem*
In a fit of rage.
The ink was still wet
On the page
As I hurled a
Soda can
At the cat.
Away she ran.

*cf. *An Unexamined Life.*

A Commissioned Omission

I can say
Almost anything
In a poem
With a zing
Except my feelings.
They don't show.
Because I don't want
You to know.

The Equinox

"Speak or be spoken to."
That's the way
I get through
The light of day.
Sometimes the night
May seem too long.
But I know
I'll get along.

Christian Ethics

To write poetry uncomplicated
Takes a simple mind.
So much I have to say,
You really should be blind.
Division by zero, they teach you,
Is still undefined.
There's nothing I want more in life
Than to be kind.

"(Proud to) Be an American"

You're a coward. I'm a "vet."
But not a veterinarian.
To my cat, I'm more like
An antiquated septuagenarian.
My sacrifice means nothing
To the madding crowd.
But it goes without saying,
I am very proud.

Criminal Minds

It is a great comfort
The world must soon end.
Everyone knows the heartache
Of losing a friend.
But the thought that they'll go on
Having a good time
As I lay dying
Is worse than a crime.

The Old Maid New

I remember when
My father said to me,
"You must take a vow
Of sacred chastity."
A Vestal virgin
I was meant to be
But never will that ever
Happen to me.

Pathology

Passive-aggressive
I may be.
But it's just
A tendency.
I'm obsessive-compulsive
The rest of the time.
Either way,
I'm in my prime.

The Messenger

From high to low, I do go,
Like a rollercoaster.
As the winds rush by, I decry
And whisper a paternoster.
If I am right, I just might,
Lose my head of hair.
And if I do, it's up to you,
To tell me it's not there.

Part III

A Bad Childhood

I was abused
When I was a child.
I was demur
Except when I was wild.
I was criticized
For everything I did.
I never want
Again to be a kid.

Abroad is a Broad

Which doctor is a witch?
Attack is a tack.
The door is ajar.
Aback is a back.
Acorn is a corn.
Appear is a pier.
Abut is a butt.
Arrear is a rear.

Taking Sides

Now is not the time
For me to celebrate
The things I love the most
And the things I love to hate.
The root of my ambivalence
Can be found within.
I have a split personality.
And I always win.

The Key of Life

It seems to me a symphony
Is comprised of cacophonous sounds.
Despite its tonal harmony,
Dissonance abounds.
To modulate to another key
They use a "pivot" chord
That transposes everything
Like chalk on a chalkboard.

Introversion

I'm happy to have
A room of my own.
I'm a recluse
In my own home.
I conduct business
Over the phone.
The truth is I'm happy
To be alone.

The Individualist

I am but
A wordy gnome
Who turns a phrase
And writes a poem.
If you like
What I have done,
You may be
The only one.

"Sixteen Candles"

They say a "Sweet Sixteen"
Is something you remember.
I remember well enough
Mine was in September.
The year eludes me now.
It was so long ago.
Just humor me if you will.
I don't want to know.

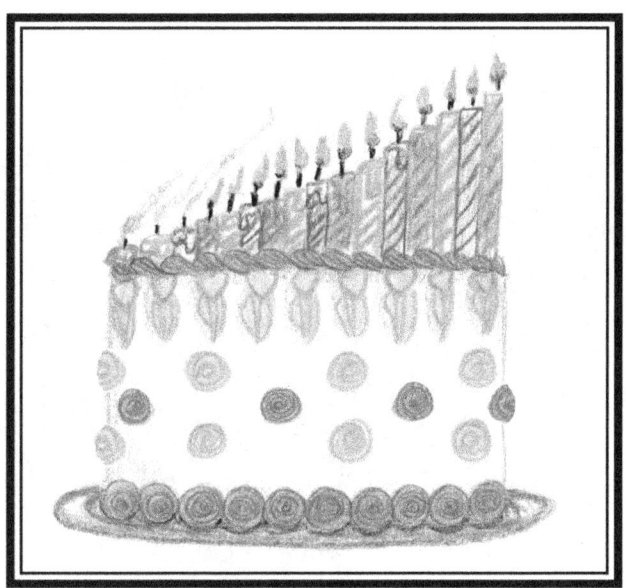

A Wrongful Death

The more doctors I see,
The sicker I get.
And never will they ever
Let me forget
To exercise strenuously
So I will be strong.
But I listen not.
I know it is wrong.

An Open Door Policy

My life is a hypocrisy.
Janus* is my name.
I'm the two-faced monster
Who everyone disdains.
It matters little to me
That everyone complains
About my "open" nature.
It's my claim to fame.

*In Greek and Roman mythology, Janus was the god of beginnings, of doorways and public places. The statue of Janus in his temple had two faces, a young one that looked toward the rising sun and an old one that faced the setting sun. At his temple in Rome, the doors were shut only in times of peace, which was extremely rare.

The Good, the Bad, and the Cogent

I can be persuasive
If I say to you
I will tell your neighbors
You dropped out of school.
But they already know
You are trying to
Conceal you servile ignorance
Using a slide rule.

"Gosh Darn It!"

Nothing is more indicative
Of your Irish charm
Than when you use an expletive
When sounding an alarm.
You mean nothing by it.
You mean no one harm.
But I can't help but think
You were raised in a barn.

A Queen Anne

Tabby thinks her Sammy
Is a sitting chair.
She tries to sit upon her
As often as she dares.
Sammy does not like it
And in anger tells her so.
But they love each other.
This much I do know.

Organ Failure

I play the organ for my church
But when I pulled the stop
The lights went dim and suddenly
I felt an electric shock.
First, my heart attacked me.
Then my kidneys, too.
I could not explain it
Nor knew not what to do.

*De profundis**

Writing, as a subject,
Is like doing a strip tease.
First you pull your top off,
Then drop down to your knees.
When you feel the first draft
Coming from the door,
You quickly put your clothes on
And then you write some more.

*Latin, "out of the depths" or pro (for) fun (the fun) of dis (disrespect) or for the fun of disrespect!

My Mistress

I was a Latin lover.
It surely changed my life.
It made me a lithe scholar
And gave to me a wife.
She doesn't do the laundry
Or cook the fatted calf.
But more importantly
She always makes me laugh.

The Bankrupted Divorcee

It only takes a moment
To let somebody know
That you really love him
And to tell him so.
If you do not do this,
You will be a cad
And will surely lose
Everything you had.

Pearl Vision

The time for change has come and gone.
I will stay the same.
I will stay the way I am.
I won't play the game.
If you don't believe me,
Then that is your loss.
Come hell or high water,
I will dental floss!

Not a Chance

You tell me you are sorry
For what you have done.
I do not believe it.
You are not the one
Who was hurt and deceived
By this little ruse.
Your apology is not accepted.
It's an offer I *can* refuse.

"Stuffed Mushrooms"

You have memorized
Every word you've read.
But for what it's worth
You may as well be dead.
What *you* bring to the party
Is really all that matters.
If I did not know better,
I'd think you all were platters.

Horse Sense

I just got my car washed.
It looks brand new
Except for the dings and scratches.
There are just a few.
But that is how I bought it
Sitting in the lot.
My judgment was impaired.
I was high on pot.

A Woman Scorned

We only hurt the ones we love.
And I hurt you bad.
I am so remorseful.
It makes me, oh, so sad
To know that you have suffered
Like a hung jury.
But there's nothing you can do,
So get over your indignant fury!

"Game Point"

What can be more swimmingly
Than to win the race.
And to do otherwise
Would be a big disgrace.
That's why I always play to win
When I play the game.
When the competition is competitive,
I am just the same.

Demigod

My destiny is manifest.
I am part divine.
Heaven sent me straight to you
In the nick of time.
You are the one
He has sent me to.
No one in the world
Means more to me than you.

"Freedom is not free"

A veteran is the kind of man,
Who kills for his country.
"A homicidal maniac."
That is pure effrontery.
"A murderer in uniform,"
The pacifist has said.
But for him we could not go
Safely to our beds.

"Suspended Animation"

Happiness may come and go.
Even sadness goes away.
Yesterday is dead and gone
And tomorrow's another day.
This I know for certain
Whatever comes my way,
There is nothing I want more from life
Than for you to stay.

Interlocution

I am a damn non sequitur
Who doesn't know her place.
A walking, talking imbecile
With no apparent grace.
I could follow anything
And I often do.
I should have listened better
When I was in school.

Eternal Bleeding

I have learned the hard way
Beauty does not last.
When I look in the mirror,
My best days are now past.
They might erase the wrinkles
Around my baggy eyes,
But they can't stop the feelings
That I now despise.

"You had me at 'Hello'"

"Guten tag! Guten Tag!"
The German says to you.
"Aloha!" and "Shalom"
Say the Hawaiian and the Jew.
But I have to say
(And this my profession),
You only get one chance
To make a first impression.

The Gift You Keep on Giving

What would you say if I went away
Never to return?
Would you cry or wonder why?
Will you ever learn?
Love is a gift you set adrift
Like the stars above,
Where you forsake everything you make
In the name of love.

Creative Orthography

If I were *are*-tistic,
I would say to you,
"I know the difference between
What is tried and what is true."
If I were *awe*-tistic,
I wouldn't say too much.
You might even say,
I was out of touch.

Continuous Discontinuity

I taught you everything I know
And some things I did not.
It matters not which is which,
You totally forgot
Everything I said to you
When you went to college.
You never know where you may go
And what passes there for knowledge.

Disorderly Conduct

Clever by half, you make me laugh
The laughter of a child.
Wherever you go, I want you to know
You drive me so wild.
But in the end, we were just friends
Of the highest order.
I must confess and do profess
I prefer disorder.

*Agnes Dei**

I had a jubilation, a joyous revelation
Of your trinity.
If it were so, where should I go
To find such ecstasy?
You are the lamb who was a man
And divinity.
Follow the star and you will go far
To achieve infinity.

*Latin, "the lamb of God," Jesus Christ. Alternate titles might be *"Hagia Sophia"* or His Holy (or Infinite) Wisdom.

Re-parenting 101

My friend is anorexic.
She thinks it's a sin.
In order to be healthy,
You have to be thin.
Sometimes I gently chide her
As she picks at her food.
But I don't force the issue
Because it would be rude.

"Hallucinogenic Spores"

Kennett Square, Pennsylvania
Is the booming capital
Of the mushroom, proud and free,
That alters the occipital.
I must say that I have watched
The boring documentary
About how mushrooms grow "soporifically"
In the local cemetery.

Fact Checking

Whenever I introduce a fact,
A specific name or place,
I must be completely accurate
Or it will egg my face.
But if, in fact, I've done it wrong
And it does not ring true,
Then I will be self-satisfied.
I have given you something to do.